BLS WORKING PAPERS

U.S. DEPARTMENT OF LABOR
Bureau of Labor Statistics

OFFICE OF EMPLOYMENT RESEARCH
AND PROGRAM DEVELOPMENT

Did Job Security Decline in the 1990s?

Jay Stewart, U.S. Bureau of Labor Statistics

Working Paper 330
August 2000

    The views expressed are those of the author and do not necessarily reflect the policies of the U.S. Bureau of Labor Statistics or the views of other staff members. This paper has benefited from conversations with Harley Frazis, Mark Loewenstein, Marilyn Manser, Jim Spletzer, and Rob Valletta. I thank two anonymous referees from their suggestions. I also thank Hank Farber, Larry Katz, David Neumark, and other participants in the Russell Sage Foundation's "Conference on Changes in Job Stability and Job Security" for their comments on an earlier version of the paper. Hector Rodriguez assisted in putting together the tables and figures.

July 6, 1999

Did Job Security Decline in the 1990s?

Jay Stewart*
Office of Employment Research
       and Program Development
Bureau of Labor Statistics
2 Massachusetts Avenue, NE
Room 4945
Voice (202) 691-7376
FAX   (202) 691-7425
E-Mail Stewart_J@BLS.GOV

* This paper has benefited from conversations with Harley Frazis, Mark Loewenstein, Marilyn Manser, Jim Spletzer, and Rob Valletta. I thank two anonymous referees for their suggestions. I also thank Hank Farber, Larry Katz, David Neumark, and other participants in the Russell Sage Foundation's "Conference on Changes in Job Stability and Job Security" for their comments on an earlier version of the paper. Hector Rodriguez assisted in putting together the tables and figures. Any opinions expressed here are mine, and do not necessarily reflect those of the Bureau of Labor Statistics.

Did Job Security Decline in the 1990s?

Jay Stewart
Office of Employment Research
and Program Development
Bureau of Labor Statistics
2 Massachusetts Avenue, NE
Room 4945
Voice (202) 606-7376
FAX (202) 606-4602
E-Mail Stewart_J@BLS.GOV

Abstract

This paper examines long term trends in job security by looking at employment-to-unemployment transitions in the March CPS. Unlike other datasets used to examine this issue, these data provide a consistently defined measure for the period covering 1967 through 1997, are available every year, and cover all workers. I find that job security appears to have declined during the early 1970s, but from the mid 1970s through the mid-to-late 1990s, there has been no change. These findings are consistent with the popular perception that jobs were less secure in the 1980s than in the 1970s, but they are not consistent with the perception that job security continued to decline in the 1990s.

I. Introduction

There has been a growing interest, both among the popular press and among researchers, in whether job stability and security have declined in recent years.[1] The popular perception is that jobs were less stable and less secure in the 1980s than in the 1970s and that this decline in stability and security continued into the 1990s.[2] So far, the evidence from academic studies indicates that job stability did not decline between the mid 1970s and the early 1990s, but that there have been changes for some groups. Job stability declined among men, primarily due to declining stability among high school dropouts.[3] Stability decreased slightly among high tenure workers.[4] For women with at least a high school diploma, job stability has increased significantly.[5]

However, the absence of a decline in job stability does not preclude declines in job security. Studies conducted so far have found that job loss appears to have been more common in the late 1980s and early 1990s than in the 1970s, and that the consequences may have become more severe. But as in the job stability debate, data quality has become an important issue.[6]

Because the primary measure of job security is the job-loss rate, most researchers have used either the Current Population Survey (CPS) Displaced Worker Supplements (DWS), the Panel Study of Income Dynamics (PSID), or the National Longitudinal Surveys (NLS). These datasets have, in principle, the correct measure, but they all have breaks in series that make it difficult to generate a consistent series over a long period (and sometimes even a short period) of time. Although researchers have devised clever ways of addressing these breaks in series, one can never be sure whether observed changes are real or due to changes in the survey instruments.

I take a different approach and use the March CPS. Although the March CPS does not have a direct measure of involuntary separations, it does contain an indirect measure that is consistently defined over a long period of time. It is well known that job losers are more likely to become unemployed and take longer to find employment than job leavers.[7] These facts suggest that I can shed additional light on the job security issue by examining trends in employment-to-unemployment (EU) transitions.

The EU transition rate is an imperfect measure of job security. Not everybody who makes an EU transition is a job loser, and not all job losers show up as having experienced an EU transition. However, later in the paper I show that the vast majority of people who experience an EU transition are job losers, and that nearly all of the variation in the EU transition rate, at least during the 1987-97 period, is due to job loss. So even though the EU transition rate does not capture all job losses, it does include the job losses policymakers are most concerned about: those resulting in unemployment. As long as the relationship between job loss that results in unemployment and the EU transition rate remains fairly constant, the EU transition rate should be a reasonable indicator of trends in job security.

There are a number of advantages to using the March CPS. First, the series is consistently defined over a long period of time (31 years), permitting longer coverage than other commonly used datasets. Since my data cover through March 1998, I can also look at very recent trends. Second, this dataset is a large nationally representative sample, making it possible to identify changes for specific demographic groups. Third, because the data are available every year, turning points can be more precisely dated.

This is not the first paper to use March CPS data to examine trends in separations. In an earlier paper (Stewart 1998), I used these data to examine trends in job stability between 1975 and 1995.[8] In that paper, I showed that it is possible to generate a reliable measure of job separations by combining the regular monthly labor force data with the data from the income supplement. I compared the labor market histories generated from the 1987 March CPS to the labor market histories generated from the 1987 January Tenure Supplement and found that the histories from the two data sources were consistent nearly 90 percent of the time. And because the questions used to identify a job separation did not change, this measure is consistently defined over the 1975-95 period. Using these data, I found that overall job stability remained constant over this period, although there were dramatic changes for some groups. In particular, job stability fell for men without a high school diploma and increased for women with more than a high school diploma.

Before continuing, it is useful to describe the findings of other researchers in the context of the data sources used and discuss some of the advantages and disadvantages of the DWS, PSID, and NLS.

The DWS

The DWS has been conducted as a supplement to the CPS every two years since 1984. It asks individuals about displacement from employers in the previous five years (1984-1992) or three years (1994-1996). The DWS has the advantage of collecting information on job loss from a large nationally representative sample. But the DWS tends to underestimate the incidence of job loss for two reasons.

First, responses are subject to recall bias. Evans and Leighton (1995) show that recall bias is severe, with the DWS underestimating displacement by about one-third. Boisjoly, Duncan, and Smeeding (1998) show that the DWS understates job loss compared to the PSID, though part of this difference appears to be a difference in concept. When they look only at job losses that resemble displacements, they get numbers that are closer to--though still larger than-- numbers from the DWS. However, because the literature on job security has focused on trends in the job-loss rate, recall bias should not be a serious problem provided it has not changed over time.[9]

The second reason is that the DWS collects information on at most one job loss, which means that it measures the number of people who experienced a job loss during the period in question, rather than the total number of job losses. Again, trend should not be affected unless the fraction of individuals with multiple job losses has changed.

The biggest drawback to using the DWS to look at recent trends in job security is that the main question changed in 1994 and again in 1996. Hence, one cannot be certain whether changes in the job-loss rate are real or due to changes in the survey, making it difficult to get a clear picture of job loss trends in the 1990s. In 1994, the reporting window was reduced from five years to three years. To illustrate how this affects responses, consider a worker who lost a job in 1993 and in 1990, with the earlier job being the longest. With a three-year window, this worker would report the 1993 job loss. If the window had been five years, the respondent could have reported either the 1990 or the 1993 job loss. If respondents always reported the most recent job loss, researchers could make the older data comparable to the more recent data simply by counting only job losses that occurred in the last three years. To the extent that respondents report the longest job lost rather than the most recent job, counting only job losses that occurred in the last 3 years would result in an underestimate of the incidence of job loss.

To address this break in series, Farber computed adjustment factors using individual labor market history data from the PSID and used those factors to adjust for the longer window in the earlier DWSs. Letting t be the current year, he calculated the fraction of workers who lost a job in year t-4 and t-5 that subsequently lost a job in years t-3 through t-1. For example, among workers who lost a job in period t-5, 27.0 percent also lost a job during the t-3 through t-1 period (the analogous rate for t-4 is 30.17 percent). The 3-year job-loss rates from the earlier data were adjusted using the following formula:

$$r_{3i}^a = r_{3i} + 0.3017\rho_{4i} + 0.2705\rho_{5i},$$

where r_{3i}^a and r_{3i} are the adjusted and unadjusted 3-year job-loss rates for group i, and ρ_{4i} and ρ_{5i} are the job-loss rates in t-4 and t-5 for group 1.

There are several problems with Farber's adjustments. First, he assumes that all multiple job losers reported the longest job lost. Bureau of Labor Statistics (BLS) research connected with the redesign of the DWS has found that about half of respondents report the most recent job lost. Second, using PSID is problematic, because the job loss concepts are not comparable (see Abraham 1997) and the PSID sample is not large enough to allow adjustment factors to vary by demographic group.[10]

In 1996, a subtle change in question wording appears to have led more quitters to show up as having lost a job. In 1994 the main question asked "During the last 3 calendar years, that is, January 1991 through December 1993, did ... lose or leave a job because: a plant or company closed or moved, (your/his/her) position or shift was abolished, insufficient work, or another similar reason?", and in 1996 the main question asked "During the last 3 calendar years, that is, January 1993 through December 1995, did ... lose a job, or leave one because: (your/his/her) plant or company closed or moved, (your/his/her) position or shift was abolished, insufficient work, or another similar reason?" Both questions ask whether "Dottie" lost or left a job, but the 1996 question places greater emphasis on leaving a job. This greater emphasis on leaving a job could have caused more job leavers to answer "Yes" to the main question. If the main question picked up more job leavers in 1996, they would most likely have shown up in the "Other" category. Given that the increase in the "Other" category drives Farber's finding of increased job loss between the 1991-93 and 1993-95 periods, it is crucial to know the extent to which the change in wording affected responses.

Research at the BLS sheds some light on this question. Abraham (1997) reports that the "Other" category is composed mostly of quitters. In response to this research, Farber (1997b) adjusted the DWS data to account for misreporting in the "Other" category in all years, and concluded that, although job loss did not increase in the 1993-95 period, it almost certainly did not decrease. However, because the debriefing questions used to determine this fact were not asked in 1994, it is impossible to directly determine whether there has been a *change* in the composition of the "Other" category. His correction is appropriate only if the 1996 wording change did not affect the composition of the "Other" category. Later in the paper, I present evidence that the change in wording did result in more job leavers answering "Yes" to the main displacement question and that it affected the non-"Other" categories.

The PSID

Several studies have used PSID data (Boisjoly, Duncan and Smeeding 1998, Polsky 1998, and Valletta 1998) to look at trends in job loss. Although the PSID collects data on job losses, it has a number of disadvantages that are worth noting. The PSID collects employment data only on household heads, so that analyses are generally restricted to male household heads. Male household heads may not be representative of all men, and are certainly not representative of the population as a whole. The sample size is relatively small, resulting in larger standard errors than in CPS data.[11] There are well documented inconsistencies in reported tenure (see Brown and Light 1992), and the tenure and job change questions have changed over time.

Dieblod, Neumark, and Polsky (1997) examined the questions used to determine turnover in the PSID and found that the wording changed. For most of the time between 1970 and 1990, the PSID asked about job changes that occurred over a 12 month period. However, from 1984 through 1987 the reporting window was closer to a year and a half (see Diebold, Neumark, and Polsky 1997 and Polsky 1998 for details). As a result, more job separations were observed in the mid 1980s simply because the window was longer. The longer window appears to have affected Boisjoly, Duncan, and Smeeding's (1998) results that job-loss rates were higher in the 1980s than in the 1970s and that job losses increased by more when looking at growth years than when looking at recession years.

To get around the problem of the longer reporting period, Polsky (1998) looked at separations using the "months in current position" question. Unfortunately, this question changed in 1983. Because the earlier question resulted in considerable heaping at 12 months and separations are detected by comparing employer tenure and the time between interviews, whether a separation is observed will be sensitive to the exact length of time between interviews. Taking advantage of the panel nature of the PSID, Polsky performed consistency checks to identify individuals who rounded up and those who rounded down. He then used the "reason for new position" question to distinguish between quits and job losses. Comparing the 1976-1981 period to the 1986-1991 period he found that there was virtually no change in job separations, but there was a large increase in the incidence of job loss conditional on a separation. Further, in comparing the late 1980s to the late 1970s, he found that job losers had become less likely to find new jobs and earned less when they did.

Valletta (1998) looked at job security in the context of an implicit contract model. He found that, for male household heads, job loss increased over the period 1976-1992, but found no such increase for women. Interestingly, the decline in job security is largest among men with higher tenure with those in declining industries faring the worst.

The NLS

A paper by Monks and Pizer (1998) used the National Longitudinal Survey of Youth (NLSY) and the NLS-YM (Young Men) to examine whether job stability and job security among young men declined between the 1970s and the 1980s.[12] They found that both voluntary and involuntary separations were more common in the 1980s than in the 1970s.

Apart from the limited sample coverage, the main difficulty with using these two datasets is that their measures of separations and job loss are not necessarily comparable. The NLS-YM asks if the individual was working two years ago[13] and what happened to that job, whereas the NLSY collects job information using a calendar approach. The latter approach is likely to detect more jobs and, hence, more job changes. Also, because the NLS-YM interviews were conducted two years apart for the years used in their study,[14] Monks and Pizer used a 2-year window to analyze job separations. To make the time period comparable in the NLSY, they used a 2-year window for these data as well. But because the NLSY interviews were conducted annually through 1994, they had to use data from two annual interviews to determine whether a separation occurred during the 2-year window of interest. It is well known that transitions are more likely to be reported between interviews than within interviews.[15] These "seam effects" imply that job separation rates should be higher in the NLSY than in the NLS-YM, even if there is no actual difference between the two cohorts. Hence, it is not clear the extent to which the 1970s-to-1980s increase in job separations found by Monks and Pizer is real and how much is due to differences in the surveys.

The rest of the paper proceeds as follows: Section II describes the data, Section III looks at the long term trends in EU transitions and compares my results to those of other studies, and Section IV concludes.

II. Data

The data used in this paper are from the 1968-1998 March CPS files. My sample consists of men and women age 19 and above in March[16] who worked at least one week in the previous year and had 40 or fewer years of potential experience.[17] Because I am interested in whether job security has changed for workers in regular (post-schooling) jobs, I omit individuals with less than one year of potential experience.[18] I also exclude self-employed workers[19] and people with zero earnings in the previous year. To simplify computation of standard errors and keep the dataset to a manageable size, I used only the first four rotation groups leaving me with a sample of 831,762 observations.[20]

As noted in the introduction, I use EU transitions as my measure of job security. It is relatively straightforward to define EU transitions in the March CPS. An individual is considered to have made an EU transition if he or she worked during the previous year and was unemployed during the reference week of March in the current year.

We know from the literature on job displacement that job losers are more likely to become unemployed and spend more time unemployed than workers who did not lose a job (see Ruhm 1991 and Farber 1993), suggesting that a large fraction of EU transitions are due to job loss. However, for the purpose of examining trends in job security, it is more important that most of the year-to-year variation in the EU transition rate be due to job loss. Fortunately, I can shed some light on this issue by using more detailed data available in the 1988 through 1998 March CPS files, which contain information on the reason for unemployment.

Over the 1988-1997 period most EU transitions were due to job losses. The EU transition rate averaged 4.65 percent over this period, with job loss accounting for 3.11

percentage points, quitters (job leavers) accounting for 0.63 percentage points, and reentrants accounting for 0.91 percentage points.[21]

The next step is to determine how much of the variation in the EU transition rate is due to job loss. Figure 1 shows the overall EU transition rate, the EU job-loss rate (this rate is the fraction of workers who worked in the previous year and were unemployed in March because of a job loss), and the EU non-job-loss rate (this rate is the fraction of workers who worked in the previous year and were unemployed in March for reasons other than job loss) for 1987-1997. It is clear from this figure that virtually all of the variation in the EU transition rate can be accounted for by variation in the EU job-loss rate.

This observation is confirmed when the 11 yearly observations are used to regress the overall EU transition rate on the EU job-loss rate. The estimated coefficient estimate on the EU job-loss rate is 0.97, which is statistically different from zero at the 1-percent level but not statistically different from one at any conventional level of significance (the R^2 on this regression is 0.96). Regressing the EU transition rate EU non-job-loss rate yields a coefficient of 0.40, which is not statistically different from zero at any conventional level of significance (the R^2 for this regression is 0.01).[22] These regressions imply that changes in the EU job-loss rate account for about 96 percent of the year-to-year variation in the EU transition rate over the 1987-97 period and suggest that the EU transition rate is a reasonable measure of job security.

It is important for my analysis that the relationship between job loss and EU transitions be fairly constant over time. For example, if workers have become more inclined to quit a job to become unemployed the EU transition rate will increase even if there has been no decline in job security. The maintained assumption throughout the rest of the paper is that this relationship was constant over the 1967-1986 period as well.

Potential Breaks in Series

There have been two changes in the CPS that could lead to potential breaks in series. The first occurred in 1989 when the Census Bureau changed the CPS processing system. Beginning in 1989, the Census changed the criteria by which variables were allocated and began imputing entire Income Supplement records using a hot deck procedure (these are known as "Type A" allocations and represent 8-10 percent of the sample). Since the Type A allocated records generate a large number of spurious transitions, I omitted them from my sample.

The second change occurred in 1994, when the Basic CPS was completely overhauled and computer assisted interviewing was introduced. The variable that is a potential problem is Employment Status Recode from the Basic CPS (ESR) [PEMLR in the New CPS]. Research by Polivka and Miller (1998) provides some guidance on how the redesign affected the ESR. They compute adjustment factors for various labor force indicators by demographic characteristics. While I cannot use these factors to adjust my estimates, they do provide useful information about which groups were most affected. The redesigned CPS detects more unemployment among both men and women. However, the largest increases in the unemployment rate are for men 65+ and women 55+. My restriction to workers with 40 or less years of potential experience largely eliminates these older workers from my analysis. Hence, any effects of the redesign are likely to be small.

III. Has Job Security Declined?

As noted in the introduction, the popular perception is that jobs were less secure in the 1980s than in the 1970s and that the decline in job security continued into the 1990s. In this section, I examine whether trends in the EU transition rate are consistent with these perceptions.

The EU transition rates in Figures 2-8 were estimated using a two step procedure. In the first step, I estimated a probit equation using only data for 1967 and obtained the predicted EU transition rate for 1967. I then estimated a probit on the full sample using year dummies (with 1967 being the reference year).[23] The EU transition rate for each year (1968 through 1997) was obtained by adding the marginal effect of the year dummy to the predicted 1967 transition rate obtained from the first step probit. To derive the upper and lower bounds of the confidence interval, I took a simple average of the standard errors on the year dummies from the second step probit and multiplied by two. These bounds were used for all years, including 1967.

Figure 2 shows the EU transition rates for all workers, men, and women. As one would expect, these series are counter-cyclical, with the EU transition rate for men exhibiting much wider swings. The EU transition rates for men and women were fairly close to each other in the late 1960s and early 1970s. The rate for both men and women ratcheted up during the 1970 and 1974 recessions, but the 1974 increase was much larger for men than for women. From the late 1970s through the mid 1990s, the EU transition rates remained roughly constant except for cyclical variation. The behavior of these EU transition rates is consistent with the popular perception that jobs were less secure in the 1980s than in the 1970s, but it is not consistent with the perception that job security declined in the 1990s. However, topside numbers can be misleading because they mask changes in composition and within group changes. Below, I present a more detailed look by demographic characteristics with the goal of determining whether job security has declined for some groups.

EU Transitions By Sex and Education

Figures 3 shows the trends in the EU transition rate for men by education level. As one might expect, the cyclical fluctuations are greater for high school dropouts and high school graduates than for workers with some college and college graduates. However, the EU transition rate for all education groups ratcheted up during the 1970 and 1974 recessions with the rates for less educated workers increasing the most. Comparing high school dropouts and high school graduates, there was a slight difference in the timing of these changes. Most of the increase among high school dropouts occurred during the 1970 recession, whereas among high school graduates most of the increase occurred during the 1974 recession. From the late 1970s through the mid 1990s, the EU transition rate for men of all education levels remained roughly constant except for cyclical fluctuations.

The corresponding EU transition rates for women are shown in Figure 4. For high school dropouts and high school graduates the patterns are similar to those for men, except that the changes are small relative to their standard errors. Like the men in these education categories the EU transition rates for women ratcheted up during the 1970 and 1974 recessions, but the increases were not as sharp. After the 1974 recession, the EU transition rate exhibited no upward or downward trend. For women with some college and college graduates there do not appear to have been any changes over the entire 1967-97 period. Again, the movements in the series are small relative to their standard errors.

In light of the debate over whether job security declined in the early 1990s, it is interesting to compare the 1982 and 1990 recessions. Although the drop in GDP was greater in the 1982 recession, the EU transition rate for male college graduates--a group that is typically insulated from cyclical job loss--was about the same in both recessions. In contrast, the EU transition rates for men in the other education groups were lower in the 1990 recession.

EU Transitions By Sex and Potential Experience

The EU transition rate for men and women by years of potential experience are shown in

Figures 5 and 6. At all levels of experience, the rates for women exhibit considerably less cyclical fluctuation than the rates for men. For men and women of all experience levels, the EU transition rate ratcheted up during the 1970 and 1974 recessions. Again, the increases were much larger for men than for women. For men with more than 10 years of experience the rates ratcheted up again during the 1982 recession. For all other groups, the EU transition rate remained relatively constant from about the mid 1970s through the mid-to-late 1990s.

Again, the 1990 recession was different from the 1982 recession for workers who are usually insulated from cyclical job loss. For men with 21 or more years of experience, the EU transition rate was as high during the 1990 recession as it was during the 1982 recession.

EU Transitions By Industry and Occupation

Figure 7 shows the EU transition rates for goods producing and services producing industries. Not surprisingly, the EU transition rate for goods producing industries exhibits much wider cyclical swings. Again, the EU transition rate for both industry groups ratcheted up during the 1970 and 1974 recessions, but remained relatively flat from the mid 1970s through the late 1990s. Comparing the 1982 and 1990 recessions, the later recession was less severe in goods producing industries, but there was no difference between the two recessions in services producing industries.

The EU transition rates in Figure 8 reveal some interesting patterns by major occupation group.[24] Note that these graphs begin in 1970 because occupation codes used in the 1968-1970 March CPS files are not compatible with the 1970 and later Census occupation codes. As expected, the EU transition rate for blue collar workers exhibits much wider cyclical swings than the rates for the other two groups. In all occupations, the EU transition rate ratcheted up during the 1974 recession, with the increase being larger for blue collar workers. A comparison of the

-14-

1982 and 1990 recessions reveals a familiar pattern. For blue collar occupations, the 1990 recession was much less severe than the 1982 recession, but for white collar occupations there was no difference between the two recessions.

Because business cycle effects can make it difficult to distinguish trends from cyclical effects in these figures, I compared average EU transition rates for the five expansions and four recessions covered by my data.

Table 1 summarizes the trends in EU transition rates for the different groups. Each line contains the results from a separate probit equation and corresponds a graph in Figures 2-8. I divided the 1967-97 period into 5 expansion periods (1967-69, 1971-73, 1976-80, 1983-89, and 1992-1997) and 4 recession periods (1970, 1974-75, 1981-82, and 1990-91) and then defined dummy variables corresponding to each of these periods (1967-69 was the omitted period). The coefficients in the first four columns correspond to expansion years, while the coefficients in the second four columns correspond to recession years. The coefficients on these dummies are expressed as marginal effects. As before, all equations include demographic control variables.

The results in Table 1 are consistent with Figures 2-8. These coefficients indicate that the EU transition rate ratcheted up in the 1970 and 1974 recessions and remained high from the late 1970s through the late 1990s. For nearly every group there were statistically significant increases in the EU transition rate between the 1967-69 and the 1971-73 periods, and for every group the increases were statistically significant between the 1971-73 and 1976-80 periods. In the last three periods (1976-80, 1983-89, and 1992-97), the EU transition rates remained relatively constant. Even when the EU transition rates are statistically different from each other, the differences are small in economic terms.

Overall, and for most groups, the 1982 recession was more severe than the 1990 recession. These differences are statistically significant at the 5-percent level. However, for a few groups there is no statistically significant difference between the EU transition rates during the two recessions. As noted above, these are groups that are normally insulated from cyclical job loss: men with college degrees, men with 21 or more years of experience, and white collar workers.

Although the behavior of the EU transition rate differs somewhat by demographic characteristics, a clear picture emerges. Job security declined during the 1970s. However, most of this decline was concentrated in the early part of the decade. The EU transition rate ratcheted up during the 1970 and 1974 recessions, but remained fairly constant after that. There is no evidence that job security continued to decline in the 1990s. These findings are consistent with the popular perception that jobs were more secure in the 1970s than in the 1980s but not with the perception that job security continued to decline in the 1990s.

Part of the reason for the inconsistency between the evidence and popular perceptions may be that the 1990 recession had a differential effect on different groups. Neumark and Polsky (1998) have suggested that reporters may have written more articles about worker displacement because a relatively large fraction of their peers--managerial and professional workers--had lost jobs. The evidence presented here is consistent with that hypothesis. Groups that are usually insulated from cyclical job loss were relatively harder hit by the 1990 recession. Even though the decline in GDP was less severe in this recession than in the 1982 recession, the EU transition rate for these insulated groups was about the same in the two recessions. In contrast, the 1990 recession was far less severe for groups that are typically less insulated from cyclical job loss.

Comparisons to Other Research

In this section I use the March CPS data to replicate, to the extent possible, the results of three other studies: Boisjoly, Duncan, and Smeeding (1998), Farber (1997a), and Monks and Pizer (1998). I seek to determine if the results presented above are consistent with these studies and to reconcile differences wherever possible.

Boisjoly, Duncan, and Smeeding (1998)

The sample used by Boisjoly, Duncan, and Smeeding consisted of male household heads aged 25-59 who had at least one year of tenure and worked at least 1,000 hours in the previous year. I was able to impose the demographic restrictions but not the tenure and hours restrictions. Hence, the March CPS sample is composed of individuals who have a weaker labor force attachment than those in the PSID sample. As a result, the job-loss rates from the PSID are lower than the EU transition rate from the March CPS.

Figure 9 shows the EU transition rate from the March CPS data and the job-loss rate from the PSID. The two series generally follow a very similar pattern, though they differ somewhat with respect to the timing of changes. Perhaps the most notable of these differences is that the EU transition rate fell between 1983 and 1987, whereas the job-loss rate from the PSID increased. This could be, at least in part, due to the longer recall period during those years.[25] Even so, their results are generally consistent with those from the March CPS.

Farber (1997a)

In replicating Farber's results with the CPS data, the difficulty was with constructing a comparable measure of EU transitions, not with replicating the sample. I computed average 3-year EU transition rates from the March CPS that are roughly comparable to Farber's 3-year job-loss rates from the DWS.[26] Because Farber's job-loss rate measures the fraction of workers that experienced a job loss during each 3-year period, I computed 3-year EU transition rate by summing the EU transition rates for the three individual years. To replicate the effect of recall bias, the rates for each year were weighted using the implied adjustment factors in Evans and Leighton (1995).[27] I also omitted the "Other" category from the DWS job-loss rates because of the problems with this category that I noted in the introduction. Figure 10 compares the 3-year EU transition rates from the March CPS to the 3-year job-loss rates from the DWS for all workers.[28]

The two series tell qualitatively the same story until the 1993-95 period. But between the 1991-93 period and the 1993-95 period the EU transition rate fell, while the job-loss rate remained roughly constant. Whether the job-loss rate fell during this period is important for determining the trend in job security in the 1990s. The natural expectation is for the job-loss rate to fall as the labor market recovers from the recession. But if, as Farber claims, the job-loss rate did not fall then that would be evidence of a permanent decline in job security.

The divergence in the 1993-95 period does not necessarily imply that the two data sources are inconsistent with each other. In particular, Farber found that the consequences of job loss became less severe between the 1991-93 and 1993-95 periods. Reemployment rates for job losers increased and their earnings losses fell.

The results from the DWS and the March CPS are consistent with two hypotheses. The first is that the job-loss rate did not fall, but instead the consequences of job loss--reemployment rates and earnings losses--were less severe during this period. The second is that the job-loss rate did fall, but that the wording change in the 1996 DWS caused more job leavers to be classified as job losers, even among the non-"Other" categories. In that case, the milder consequences of job loss that Farber found would be due to the higher fraction of job leavers that were misclassified as lob losers.

Recall that the main question in the 1996 DWS placed greater emphasis on leaving a job than did the 1994 question. It has been hypothesized that this wording change resulted in more job leavers answering "Yes" to the main question and that it accounts for the large increase in the "Other" category in the 1996 DWS. But it is possible that some job leavers who answered "Yes" to the main question gave a reason other than "Other."

Although it is not possible to determine what reason these job leavers might have given, the "Insufficient work" category seems like a likely candidate because it may not be clear what the phrase means. It was intended to describe a situation in which an employee was terminated because his employer had experienced a decline in demand. But respondents may have interpreted the term to include situations in which the worker left a job voluntarily because he wanted to work more hours or there was not enough work to keep him busy.

Research associated with the redesign of the DWS has shown that a large fraction of people in the "Insufficient work" category are actually job leavers. The 1996 and 1998 DWSs included a set of debriefing questions that were designed to determine whether respondents were answering the questions correctly.[29] When they analyzed the data, BLS researchers found that 32 percent of people who gave "Insufficient work" as a reason were job leavers. Of these, only 38 percent left because they expected their job to end. Hence, a relatively large fraction --20 percent--were true job leavers. In contrast, about 14 percent of people who said that they had lost a job due to "Plant closing" or "Position abolished," which are less ambiguous terms, were actually job leavers. Approximately two-thirds of these job leavers said that they left because they expected their job to end, so that less than 5 percent of individuals in these two categories were true job leavers.

However, the real issue is whether this type of misreporting became more common between the 1994 and 1996 DWS. Unfortunately, there were no follow-up questions in the 1994 DWS, so a direct test is not possible. However, it is possible to perform a consistency check by determining whether the increase in the reemployment rate for job losers in the DWS was large enough to reconcile Farber's finding of no change in job-loss rates with my finding of a decline in the EU transition rate.

My strategy is to estimate a lower bound on the amount by which the reemployment rate must have increased in order for Farber's results to be consistent with mine. If the change in the reemployment rate from the DWS is less than this lower bound, it would be evidence that the 1996 DWS classified a higher fraction of job leavers as job losers than the 1994 DWS. Because the reemployment rates from the DWS cover a 3-year period and the EU transition rates from the March CPS cover approximately a 1-year period, the levels are not comparable. Instead I compare the percentage changes in the reemployment rates from the two surveys.

Let me begin with the following identity:

(1) $$P_L \equiv P_{LU} + P_{LN} + P_{LE},$$

where P_L is the fraction of employed workers who lose a job over the course of a year, P_{LU} is the fraction that loses a job and becomes unemployed, P_{LN} is the fraction that loses a job and leaves the labor force, and P_{LE} is the fraction that loses a job and becomes reemployed.

Computing the percentage change in P_{LE} from the DWS was straightforward. I used Farber's estimates of P_{LE} from the DWS to compute the percentage change between the 1991-93 and 1993-95 periods.[30] As before, I excluded the "Other" category from my calculations. The reemployment rate (expressed as a fraction of employment)[31] increased from 6.4 percent to 6.7 percent, an increase of 5.3 percent.

It is more difficult to compute the percentage change in P_{LE} from the March CPS data because P_{LE} cannot be estimated directly. In fact, of the variables in Equation (1), I can only estimate P_{LU} (using the reason for unemployment question). For the other variables, it is necessary to obtain estimates from other sources or make assumptions about their values.

For some of the variables, it is easier to make assumptions about the changes than the levels. Taking the difference between the 1991-1993 and 1993-95 periods yields

$$(2) \qquad \Delta P_L \equiv \Delta P_{LU} + \Delta P_{LN} + \Delta P_{LE}.$$

As noted above, I can estimate ΔP_{LU} directly from the March CPS data. By assumption, ΔP_L is close to zero. Given that $\Delta P_{LU} < 0$ (from the March CPS) and $\Delta P_{LE} > 0$ (from the DWS), the labor market must have been improving. Hence, it is reasonable to suppose that $\Delta P_{LN} < 0$. Since smaller (more negative) values of ΔP_{LN} increase the lower bound on the percentage change in P_{LE}, I take the conservative approach and assume $\Delta P_{LN} = 0$.

For both three-year periods, my estimate of P_{LU} was calculated by taking the number of people who made EU job-loss transitions and dividing by the number of people who worked at all during the previous year (2.74 percent in 1991-93 and 2.10 percent in 1993-95). I adjusted my estimates of P_{LU} to account for recall bias (as described above) and the 1994 redesign of the CPS. For the latter adjustment, I used adjustment factors from Polivka and Miller (1998) to account for the fact that the redesigned CPS classifies a smaller fraction of the unemployed as job losers.[32]

For my estimates of P_L, I used the job-loss rates from the DWS (9.6 percent in 1991-93 and 9.5 percent in 1993-95). This is a conservative approach, because the percentage change in the reemployment rate decreases as P_L increases[33] and the DWS job-loss rate (which is a three-year rate) is an overestimate of the average annual job-loss rate.[34] Because I had no way of estimating P_{LN}, I performed the calculations using assumed values that ranged from zero to two percent (which would be about 20 percent of all job losers). My estimate of the initial value of P_{LE} was calculated by plugging these values into Equation (1).

The results of these calculations are presented in Table 2. The first four columns show the values of the variables from Equation (1), while the second four columns show the changes in these variables between 1991-93 and 1993-95 from Equation (2). Using the most conservative estimate ($P_{LN} = 0$ in the 1991-93 period), the reemployment rate for job losers would had to have increased by at least 7.7 percent--compared with the actual increase of 5.3 percent in the DWS--for the small decline in the job-loss rate observed in the DWS to be consistent with the EU job-loss rate from the March CPS. If one makes the more reasonable assumption that $P_{LN} = 1$ in 1991-93, (or about 10 percent of job losers), then the implied percentage increase in the reemployment rate is 9.2 percent, well above the DWS estimate.

Hence, these calculations support the hypothesis that the job-loss rate actually decreased between the 1991-1993 and 1993-95 periods and that the change in the DWS resulted in more job leavers being classified as job losers than in previous years.

These calculations also illustrate the potential danger of trying to examine trends when the underlying data collection instrument has changed. The raw data seem to indicate that job security fell during the mid 1990s. But further examination shows that this finding was most likely caused by a change in the questionnaire rather than a true change in job security.

Monks and Pizer (1998)

The sample used by Monks and Pizer was restricted to young men in two NLS cohorts--

one aged 19-27 in 1971 and one aged 19-27 in 1984--who were working full time (at least 30 hours per week) in the following years: 1971, 1973, 1976, and 1978 (from the NLS-YM) and 1984, 1985, 1989, and 1990 (from the NLSY). I was able to impose the cohort and sample year restrictions, but not the full-time restriction.[35]

As noted in the introduction, Monks and Pizer determined whether a job separation occurred in the 2-year period following each sample year and whether the separation was involuntary. Because the March CPS data measure EU transitions over a 14.5 month window, I used data for each of their starting years plus the following year: 1971-74 and 1976-79 for the NLS-YM cohorts and 1984-86 and 1989-91 for the NLSY cohorts.[36]

I estimated Monks and Pizer's probit equations for involuntary separations (see their Table 6) using March CPS data. The main variables of interest are the set of education dummy variables interacted with a time trend variable.[37] My results were qualitatively very similar to theirs for the control variables, but there were some differences in the coefficients on the main variables of interest.

Tables 3 and 4 compare the results on the main variables of interest from the two datasets. Table 3 compares the coefficients from probit equations on the EU transition rate (from the March CPS) and the job-loss rate (from the NLS) for both whites and nonwhites. Both data sources indicate that there were large and statistically significant increases in the job-loss rate (NLS) and the EU transition rate (March CPS) among high school dropouts and high school graduates. Among men with some college and college graduates, the NLS data show large and statistically significant increases in the job-loss rates for whites, but not for nonwhites. In contrast, for both whites and nonwhites the March CPS data show no change in the EU transition rate among men with some college and college graduates.

To better compare the magnitude of the estimated changes, I compared the 1971-to-1991 changes implied by the point estimates. These changes, which are expressed as percentage changes to make them more comparable, are shown in Table 4.[38]

Among whites, the two data sources tell identical stories for high school dropouts and high school graduates, but differ significantly when it comes to people with more than a high school diploma. Both data sources show that the probability of a job loss/EU transition increased by about 75 percent among white high school dropouts and by about 50 percent among white high school graduates. In the some college and college graduates categories, the NLS shows a much larger increase in the probability of a job loss than the March CPS. For the some college category the job-loss rate increased by 100 percent in the NLS, compared with a 13-percent increase in the EU transition rate in the March CPS. For college graduates, the increases were 65 percent in the NLS and 11 percent in the March CPS.

The differences between the two data sources are even greater for nonwhites. For high school dropouts the increase in the March CPS data was twice that in the NLS data, while for high school graduates the reverse was true. I hesitate to say much about the other two education categories because none of the changes are statistically significant.

It is not clear why the two surveys tell such different stories, but differences in survey design between the NLS-YN and the NLSY are probably not the cause. If they were the cause, then one would expect the NLS to indicate uniformly larger increases in probabilities between 1971 and 1990. The fact that the NLS and the March CPS produced very similar results for some education groups but not for others suggests that something else is going on.

V. Summary and Conclusions

The evidence presented here suggests that job security, as measured using EU transition rates, declined in the early to mid 1970s and, except for cyclical fluctuations, remained constant through the mid 1990s. This finding is consistent with the popular perception that jobs were less secure in the 1980s than in the 1970s, but not with the perception that job security continued to decline in the 1990s. A more detailed look at the EU transition rate for different demographic groups does not change this conclusion, but it does shed some light on how the perception that job security declined in the 1990s may have come about.

The 1990 recession was more "white collar" than previous recessions. Neumark and Polsky (1998) hypothesized that reporters may have written more articles about worker displacement because a relatively large fraction of their peers had lost jobs. The evidence presented here is consistent with that hypothesis. Groups that are usually insulated from cyclical job loss--such as men with a college degree, men with more labor market experience, and white collar workers--were relatively harder hit by the 1990 recession. The EU transition rates for these groups were about the same in both the 1982 and 1990 recessions, even though the 1990 recession was far less severe in terms of the decline in GDP. In contrast, the EU transition rates for less educated men, less experienced men, and blue collar workers were much lower in the 1990 recession than in the 1982 recession.

It is also possible that the slow recovery from the 1990 recession contributed to this perception. Even though the recession officially ended in March 1991, the labor market did not begin to recover until much later. The EU transition rate peaked in 1991, but remained high through 1992. The unemployment rate did not peak until 1992, and job growth was sluggish through 1992.

The advantage of using March CPS data is that the series extends through 1997, so it is possible to distinguish between a slower than normal recovery from the 1990 recession and the start of a secular trend. The EU transition rate had returned to its pre-recession level by 1994 implying that the higher EU transition rates in the early 1990s were not the start of a secular trend. Most other studies cannot make this distinction because the data used stop in the early 1990s. Farber's (1997a) data cover through 1995, but it is problematic to make inferences about trends in the 1990s because of wording changes in the main question in the DWS.

In comparing my results to those of other authors, I found that my results were generally consistent though there were some differences worth noting.

I found that my results are generally consistent with those of Boisjoly, Duncan, and Smeeding (1998). Both the job-loss rate in the PSID and the EU transition rate in the March CPS show jobs were less secure in the 1980s compared with the 1970s. Both data sources indicate that job security declined throughout the 1970s, and remained constant or decreased slightly in the 1980s. However, by looking at only men Boisjoly, Duncan, and Smeeding tend to overstate the overall decrease in job security, because women did not experience as large a decline.

My results are similar to Farber's (1997a), except for the mid 1990s. The job-loss rate in the DWS data remained constant while the EU transition rate in the March CPS data fell. I presented evidence that the DWS job-loss rate for the 1993-95 period may have been affected by a subtle wording change in the main question. A consistency check indicates that a larger fraction of job leavers were classified as job losers in the 1996 DWS than in previous years. Hence, it appears that job-loss rates actually fell in the mid 1990s. This finding illustrates the danger of trying to examine trends when the underlying data collection instrument has changed.

I was able to replicate Monks and Pizer's results for some groups but not for others. Results from the NLS and the March CPS were close for white high school dropouts and high school graduates. In the some college and college graduate categories, Monks and Pizer found a large increase in the job-loss rate, whereas I found very little change.

References

Aaronson, Daniel and Daniel Sullivan (1998) "The Decline on Job Security in the 1990s: Displacement, Anxiety, and their Effect on Wage Growth," *Economic Perspectives*, First Quarter 1998, Federal Reserve Bank of Chicago, pp. 17-43.

Abraham, Katharine G. (1997) Comment on Farber "The Changing Face of Job Loss in the United States: 1981-1995," *Brookings Papers on Economic Activity: Microeconomics*, in press.

Bernhardt, Annette, Martina Morris, Mark Handcock, and Marc Scott (1998) "Job Instability and Wage Inequality Among Young Men: A Comparison of Two NLS Cohorts," mimeo.

Boisjoly, Johanne, Greg J. Duncan, and Timothy Smeeding (1998) "The Shifting Incidence of Involuntary Job Losses from 1968 to 1992," *Industrial Relations* 37(2), April 1998, pp. 207-31.

Brown, James N. and Audrey Light (1992) "Interpreting Panel Data on Job Tenure," *Journal of Labor Economics* 10(3), July 1992, pp. 219-57.

Diebold, Francis X., David Neumark, and Daniel Polsky (1997) "Job Stability in the United States," *Journal of Labor Economics* 15(2), April 1997, pp. 206-33.

Diebold, Francis X., David Neumark, and Daniel Polsky (1996) "Comment on Kenneth A. Swinnerton and Howard Wial, 'Is Job Stability Declining in the U.S. Economy?'"

Industrial and Labor Relations Review 49(2), January 1996, pp. 348-352.

Evans, David S. and Linda S. Leighton (1995) "Retrospective Bias in the Displaced Worker Surveys," *Journal of Human Resources* 30(2), Spring 1995, pp.386-196.

Fallick, Bruce C. (1996) "A Review of the Recent Literature on Displaced Workers," *Industrial and Labor Relations Review* 50(1), October 1996, pp.5-16.

Farber, Henry S. (1993) "The Incidence and Costs of Job Loss: 1982-1991," *Brooking Papers on Economic Activity: Microeconomics*, pp.73-132.

Farber, Henry S. (1997a) "The Changing Face of Job Loss in the United States: 1981-1995," *Brookings Papers on Economic Activity: Microeconomics*, in press.

Farber, Henry S. (1997b) "Has the Rate of Job Loss Increased Over Time?" mimeo, December 1997.

Farber, Henry S. (1998) "Are Lifetime Jobs Disappearing? Job Duration in the United States: 1973-1993," in *Labor Statistics Measurement Issues*, John Haltiwanger, Marilyn Manser, and Robert Topel, eds., University of Chicago Press.

Jacobson, Louis, Robert LaLonde, and Daniel Sullivan (1993) "Earnings Losses of Displaced Workers," *American Economic Review* 83(4), September 1993, pp. 685-709.

Jaeger, David (1997) "Reconciling the Old and New Census Bureau Education Questions: Recommendations for Researchers," *Journal of Business and Economic Statistics* 15(3), pp.300-9.

Jaeger, David and Ann Huff Stevens (1997) "Is Job Stability in the United States Falling? Trends in the Current Population Survey and Panel Study of Income Dynamics," mimeo.

Marcotte, David (1996) "Has Job Stability Declined?: Evidence from the Panel Study of Income Dynamics," mimeo.

Martini, Alberto and Paul Ryscavage (1991) "The Impact of Survey and Questionnaire Design on Longitudinal Labor Force Measures," mimeo.

Monks, James, and Steven Pizer (1997) "Trends in Voluntary and Involuntary Job Turnover," *Industrial Relations* 37(4), October 1998, pp. 440-59.

Murphy, Kevin M. and Finis Welch (1992) "The Structure of Wages," *Quarterly Journal of Economics* 107(1), February 1992, pp. 285-326.

Neumark, David and Daniel Polsky (1998) "Changes in Job Stability and Job Security: Anecdotes and Evidence" in the Proceedings of the 50th Annual IRRA Meetings.

Neumark, David, Daniel Polsky, and Daniel Hansen (1998) "Has Job Stability Declined Yet? New Evidence for the 1990s," mimeo.

Pierret, Charles (1999) "Event History Data and Survey Recall: An Analysis of the NLSY
Recall Experiment," mimeo.

Polivka, Anne E. and Steven Miller (1995) "The CPS After the Redesign: Refocusing the
Economic Lens," in *Labor Statistics Measurement Issues*, John Haltiwanger, Marilyn
Manser, and Robert Topel, eds., University of Chicago Press.

Polsky, Daniel (1996) "Changes in the Consequences of Job Separations in the U.S. Economy,"
Mimeograph, University of Pennsylvania.

Rose, Stephen (1995) "Declining Job Security and the Professionalization of Opportunity,"
National Commission for Employment Policy, Research Report 95-4, April 1995.

Ruhm, Christopher (1991) "Are Workers Permanently Scarred by Job Displacements?"
American Economic Review 81(1), March 1991, pp. 319-24.

Stewart, Jay (1998) "Has Job Mobility Increased? Evidence from the Current Population
Survey: 1975-1995," BLS Working Paper #308.

Swinnerton, Kenneth A. and Howard Wial (1995) "Is Job Stability Declining in the U.S.
Economy?" *Industrial and Labor Relations Review* 48(2) January 1995, pp. 293-304.

Swinnerton, Kenneth A. and Howard Wial (1996) "Is Job Stability Declining in the U.S.

Economy? Reply to Diebold, Neumark, and Polsky" *Industrial and Labor Relations Review* 48(2) January 1996, pp. 352-355.

Valletta, Robert (1996) "Has Job Security in the U.S. Declined?" FRBSF Weekly Letter 96-07, February 16,

Valletta, Robert (1998) "Declining Job Security" mimeo.

Endnotes

[1] *Job stability* refers to the duration of jobs, without regard to the reasons for increasing or decreasing duration. Examples of job stability measures include retention rates (Swinnerton and Wial 1995,1996, Marcotte 1996, and Diebold, Neumark, and Polsky 1996,1997, and Neumark, Polsky, and Hansen 1998), job tenure (Farber 1998), the fraction of workers in new jobs (Jaeger and Stevens 1998), and turnover (Rose 1995, Monks and Pizer 1998, and Stewart 1998). *Job security* refers to the extent to which job separations are involuntary. The primary measure of job security is the rate of job loss (Polsky 1998, Farber 1997a,b, Boisjoly, Duncan, and Smeeding 1998, Monks and Pizer 1998, and Valletta 1998).

[2] See Neumark and Polsky (1998).

[3] See Marcotte (1996), Farber (1998), and Stewart (1998). Diebold, Neumark, and Polsky (1997) found that job stability fell among less educated workers but did not present gender breaks.

[4] See Neumark, Polsky, and Hansen (1998).

[5] See Farber (1998) and Stewart (1998).

[6] See Stewart (1998) for a discussion of the data issues in the job stability literature.

[7] See Ruhm (1991). See also Fallick (1996) for a nice survey of the job displacement literature.

[8] The shorter time period was used because a key variable for identifying job separations was not available until March 1976 (covering calendar year 1975). This variable is not required to identify EU transitions.

[9] Recall bias is more of a problem if information on the year of job loss is used to determine changes in the job-loss rate within the period covered by the survey. Because more recent years

are "weighted" more heavily, increases in the job-loss rate will be overstated, while decreases will be understated. However, using three-year job-loss rates (as Farber does) minimizes the impact of this bias.

[10] Aaronson and Sullivan (1998) avoided the problem completely by restricting their analysis to workers with 5 or more years of tenure and job losses that occurred in the three years prior to the survey. They found that job-loss rates increased in the 1990s, but their analysis does not account for the 1996 change in the wording of the main question in the DWS.

[11] See Jaeger and Stevens (1998) for a comparison.

[12] In a similar analysis, Bernhardt, et al. (1998) look at job stability using NLS data.

[13] More specifically, the respondent is asked if they were working during a specific month and year about two years prior to the interview.

[14] Interviews for the NLS-YM were conducted annually from 1966 through 1971 and in the following years: 1973, 1975, 1976, 1978, 1980, 1981, 1983, and 1990. Monks and Pizer used data from 1971, 1973, 1976, and 1978 as their base years and determined whether respondents were still working at their the main (CPS) job two years later.

[15] Most of the research looking at this issue looks at SIPP data in the context of generating monthly gross flows data (for example, see Martini and Ryscavage 1991). Pierret (1999) analyzes data from an NLSY test that collects data for 1992 in both the 1993 and 1994 interviews. He finds that respondents were more likely to both forget and misremember things events from 1992 in the 1994 interview than in the 1993 interview.

[16] I used 19 rather than 18 as the cutoff because the age refers to the age at the time of the survey.

[17] I compute potential experience as Age - Years of Schooling Completed - 6 if Years of

Schooling is greater than 10 years, and as Age - 16 for those with 10 or fewer Years of Schooling Completed. This definition is used in Murphy and Welch (1992). Experience is computed for March of the previous year.

[18] I use this restriction because it is not possible to identify students and recent graduates on a consistent basis over the years covered by my data.

[19] I include wage and salary workers who have some self-employment income.

[20] Using the full sample would result in a relatively small decline in standard errors. If the observations were independent there would be a 40 percent reduction in the standard errors. But because each individual shows up twice (in consecutive years) in the full sample, it would be necessary to account for the covariance between observations making the actual reduction much smaller.

[21] It is not clear how the reentrants should be classified. These individuals lost or left a job, left the labor force, but had reentered the labor force by March. They could be job losers who became discouraged over their prospects of finding a new job, or they could be job leavers who left the labor force.

Note also that the reentrants group includes the 0.03 percent who were classified as new entrants. Presumably these new entrants were miscoded because everybody in the sample worked at some point during the previous year. For that reason (and because there are so few of them), I grouped the new entrants with the reentrants.

[22] The results did not change when I looked at job leavers and reentrants separately.

[23] All of the probit equations used for Figures 2-8 include demographic controls (dummy variables for 3 education levels, 4 experience levels, and dummy variables for race, sex, and

marital status). In the probits for subgroups, the appropriate control variables are omitted.

[24] I thank Dave Macpherson for providing me with the program used to convert the 1970 Census occupation to 1980 codes.

[25] Boisjoly, Duncan, and Smeeding did not adjust their data for the change in recall period noted in Diebold, Neumark, and Polsky (1997).

[26] Farber used three-year intervals because the DWS measures the number of people who lost at least one job in the previous three years. While the DWS identifies the year in which the job loss occurred, it is not really designed to count the number of people who lost a job in each year.

[27] Evans and Leighton (1995) found that respondents forgot job losses at a rate of about 17 percent per year. The exact adjustment factors are 0.908 for the previous year, 0.748 for the second year, and 0.616 for the third year. So to adjust the data for the 1981-82 period, the EU transition rate for 1983 was multiplied by 0.908, the EU transition rate for 1982 was multiplied by 0.748, and the EU transition rate for 1981 was multiplied by 0.616.

[28] I also compared the EU transition rate and the job-loss rates by sex, by sex and education level, and by sex and age and got qualitatively similar results.

[29] The data reported here were provided by Jim Esposito of BLS. They are from the debriefing questions in the 1998 DWS (the results are very similar to those from the 1996 DWS).

[30] The data were taken from Farber's (1997a) Tables 7 and Appendix Table 1.

[31] This measure is more intuitively described as the fraction of workers who lost a job and then found a new job.

[32] These adjustments to not affect the results. In fact, the calculated lower bounds are larger before making the adjustments for recall bias and the CPS redesign.

[33] Actually, it is a decreasing function of P_L in the initial period. But recall that, by assumption, ΔP_L is close to zero.

[34] There is the issue of recall bias, which would tend to work in the opposite direction. To check the reasonableness of using the DWS rate, I computed job-loss rates from the Basic CPS using the reason for unemployment variable. I computed the "monthly" job-loss rate as the number of permanent job losers that were unemployed for 4 or fewer weeks divided by total employment in March. To arrive at an annual number, I multiplied by 13. The estimated annual rate of .092 is an overestimate of the relevant job-loss rate because it counts multiple job losers more than once.

[35] The required hours data are not available until the March 1976 CPS.

[36] The results do not qualitatively change if only the sample years are used.

[37] In addition to the main variables of interest, their equation included three dummy variables for education level, the average unemployment rate, age at time of interview, marital status, and dummy variables for industry and occupation. They also included a variable to account for differences in the time between the initial interview and the interview approximately two years later. I did not include this variable because there is so little variation in the time between interviews in the CPS.

[38] Steve Pizer kindly provided the probabilities from the NLS.

Figure 1: EU Transition Rates by Reason for Unemployment

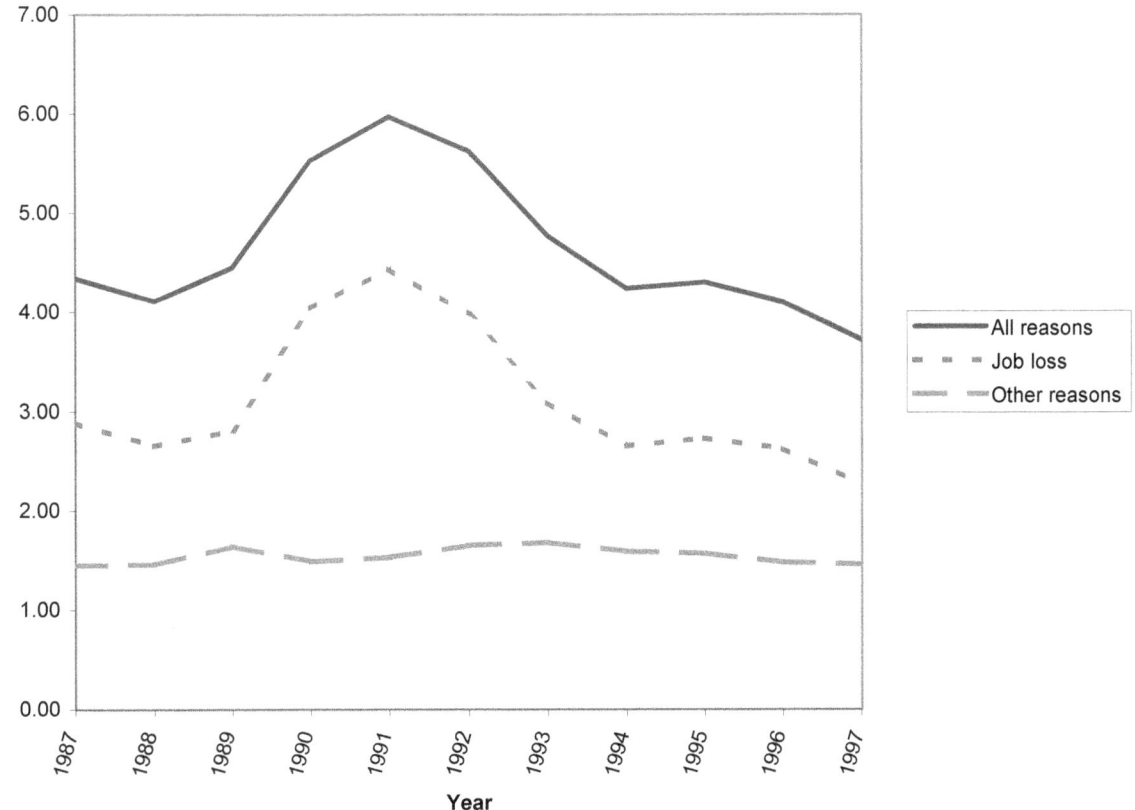

Figure 2: EU Transition Rates for All Workers, Men, and Women

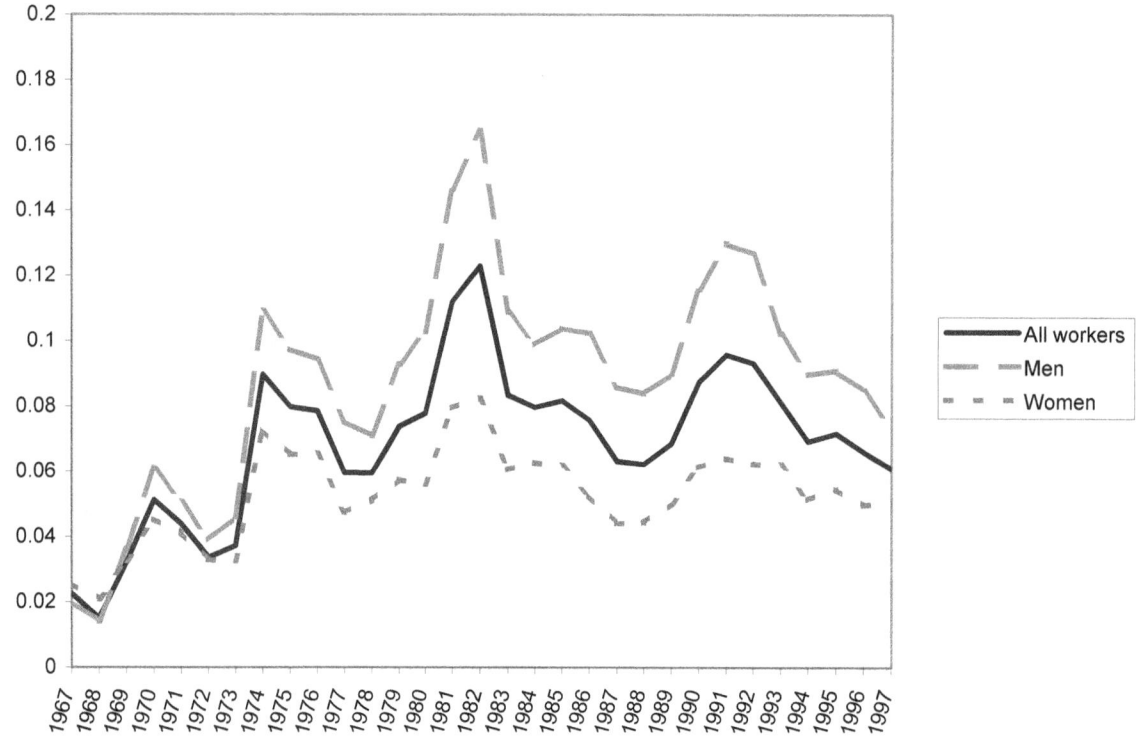

Figure 3: EU Transition Rates for Men by Educational Level

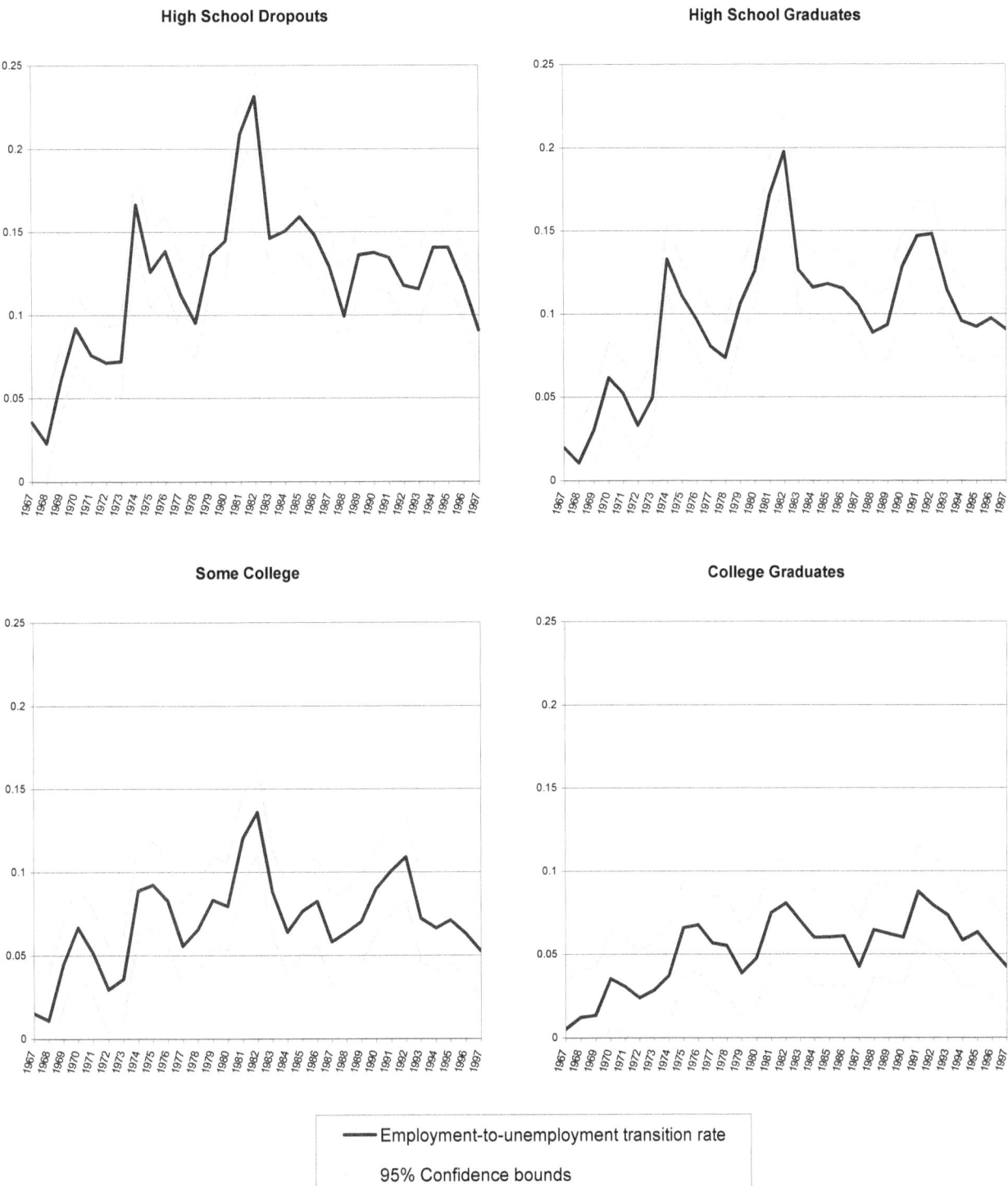

Figure 4: EU Transition Rates for Women by Education Level

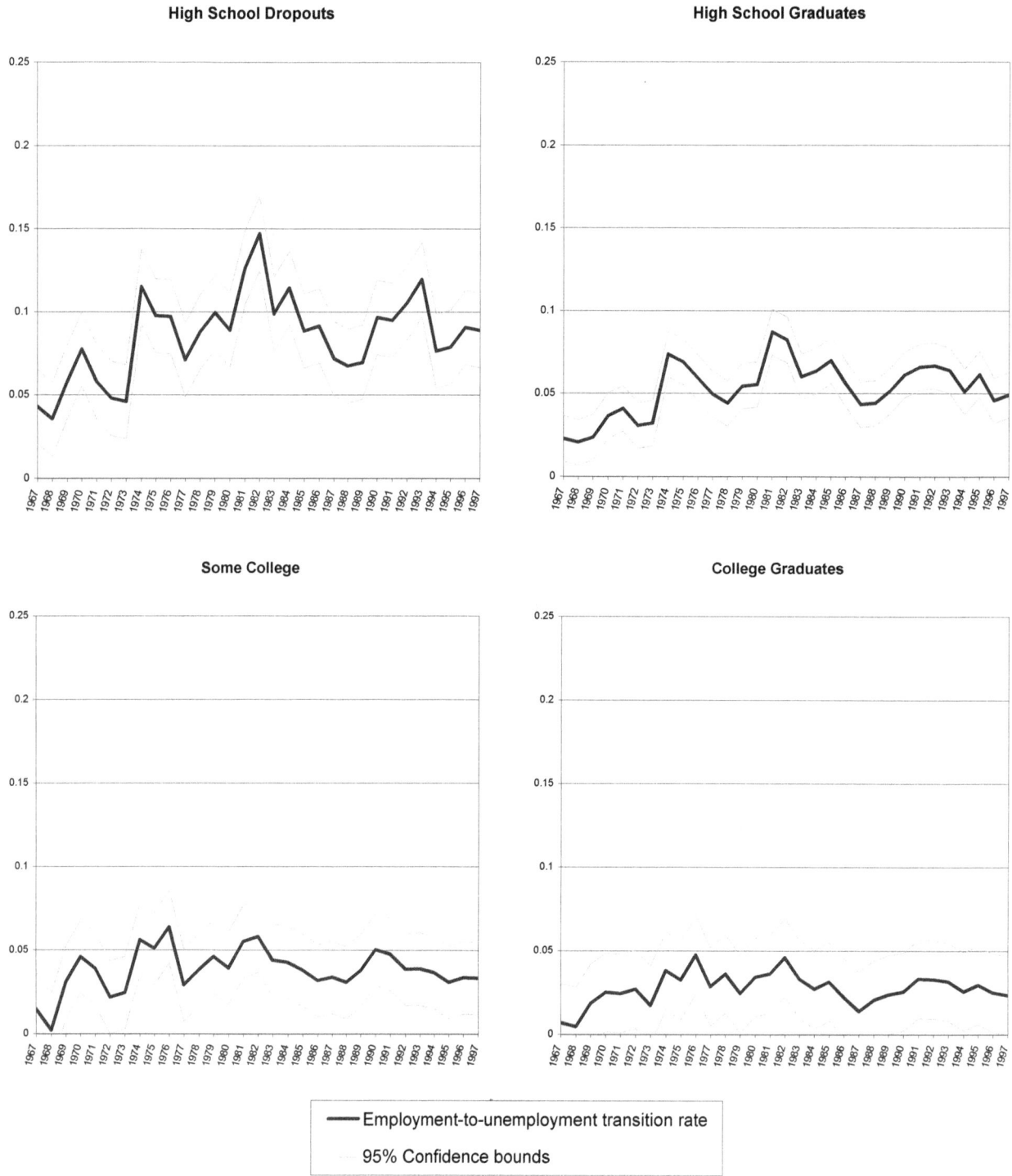

Figure 5: EU Transition Rates for Men by Years of Potential Experience

1 - 10 Years of Potential Experience

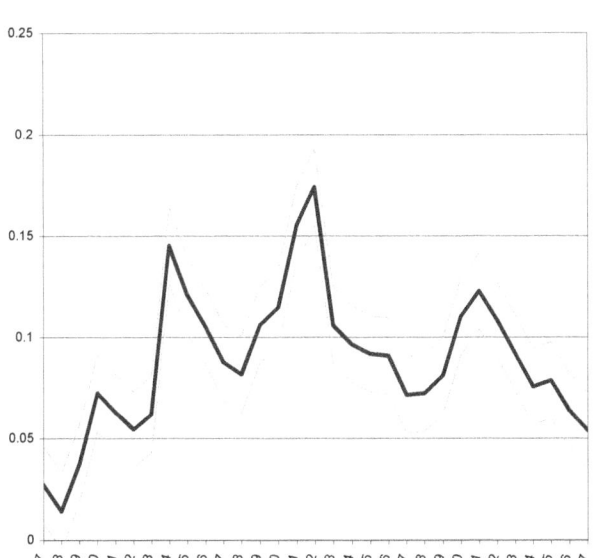

11 - 20 Years of Potential Experience

21 - 30 Years of Potential Experience

31 - 40 Years of Potential Experience

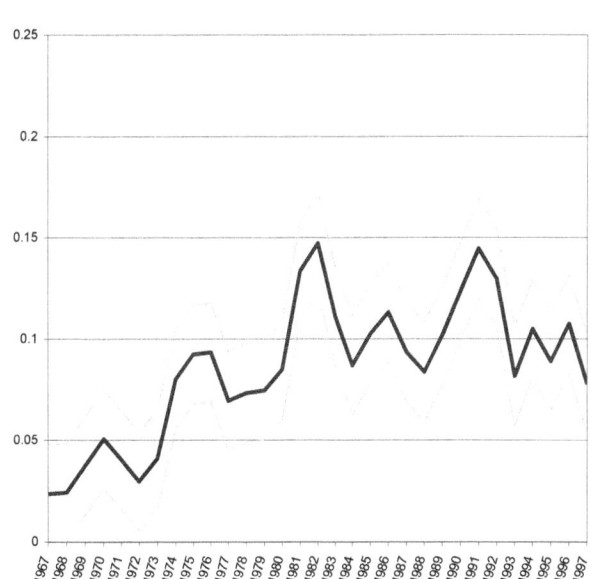

——— Employment-to-unemployment transition rate

95% Confidence bounds

Figure 6: EU Transition Rates for Women by Years of Potential Experience

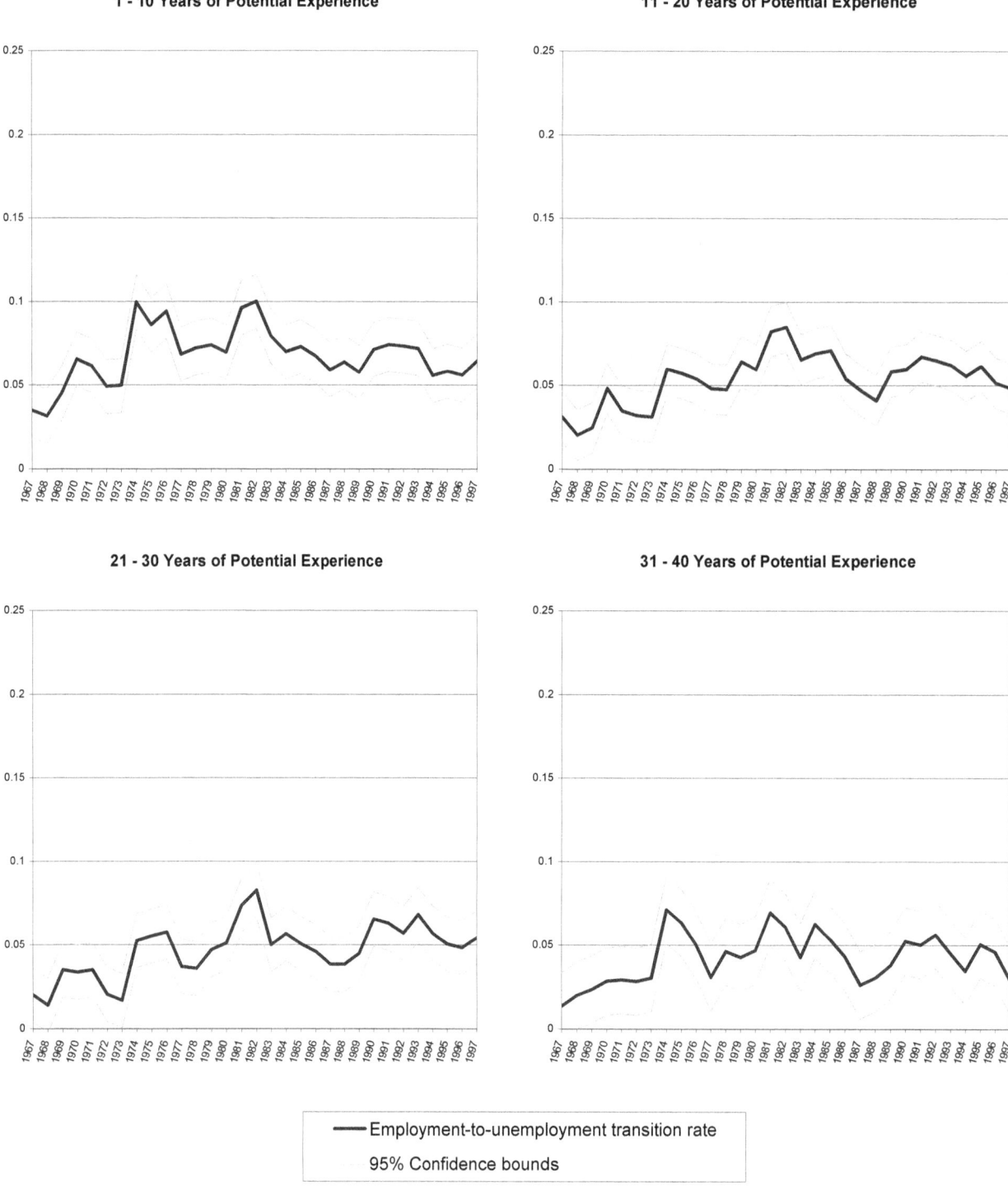

Figure 7: EU Transitions by Major Industry Group

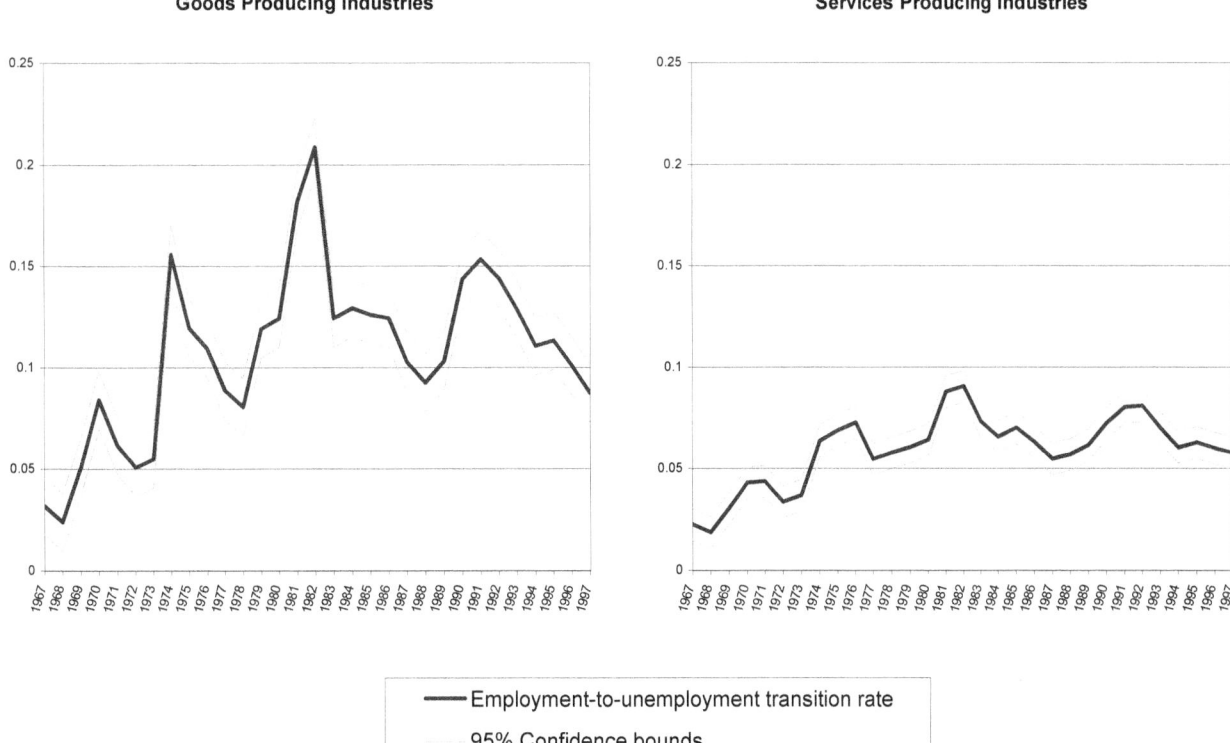

Goods Producing Industries

Services Producing Industries

——— Employment-to-unemployment transition rate

95% Confidence bounds

Figure 8: EU Transitions by Major Occupation Group

White Collar Occupations

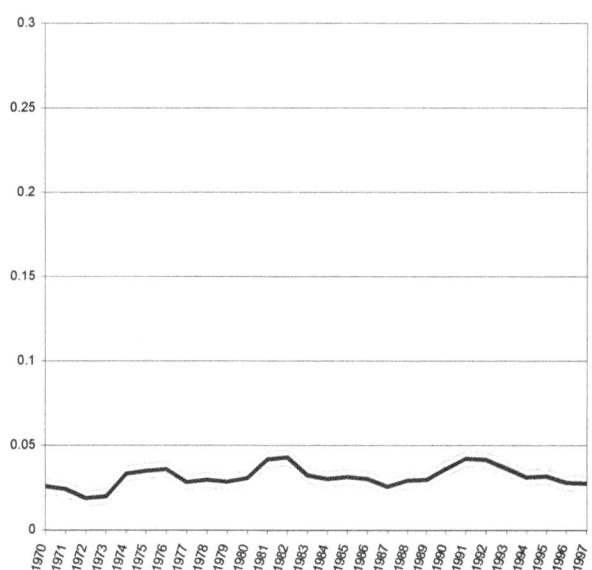

Blue Collar Occupations

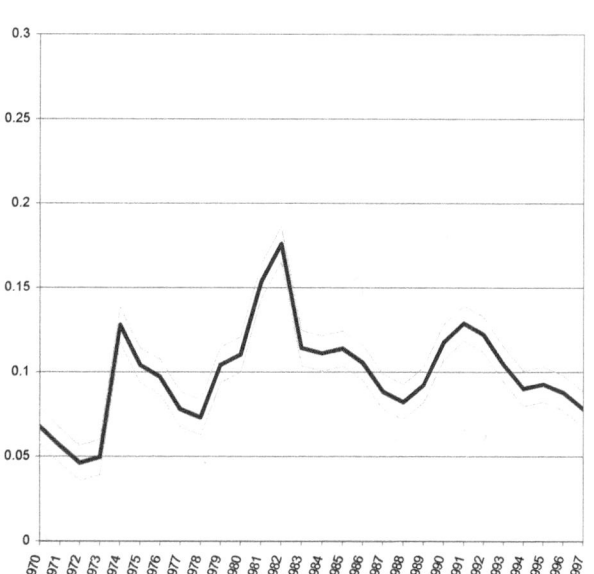

Service Occupations

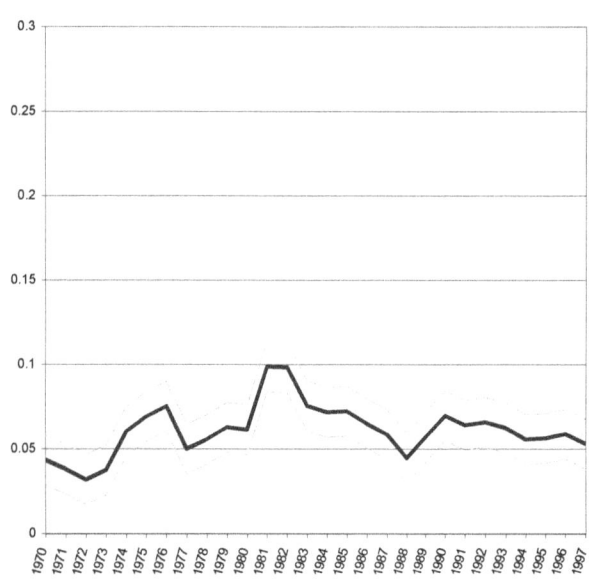

Employment-to-unemployment transition rate

95% Confidence bounds

Table 1. Probit Estimates of Changes in EU Transition Rates for Expansion Years and Recession Years

	Expansion Years				Recession Years				Observations
	1971 - 73	1976 - 80	1983 - 89	1992 - 97	1970	1974 - 75	1981 - 82	1990 - 91	
All Workers	0.0152*	0.0428*	0.0436*	0.0456	0.0279	0.0596*	0.0895*	0.0654*	831,762
	(0.0015)	(0.0016)	(0.0016)	(0.0016)	(0.0023)	(0.0023)	(0.0026)	(0.0023)	
Men	0.0207*	0.0564*	0.0604*	0.0623	0.0360	0.0754*	0.1226*	0.0929*	450,297
	(0.0022)	(0.0024)	(0.0022)	(0.0025)	(0.0034)	(0.0035)	(0.0040)	(0.0037)	
Women	0.0091*	0.0271*	0.0247	0.0265	0.0187	0.0415*	0.0528*	0.0354*	381,465
	(0.0020)	(0.0020)	(0.0018)	(0.0019)	(0.0030)	(0.0030)	(0.0030)	(0.0027)	
Men by Education Level:									
High school dropouts	0.0335*	0.0792*	0.0929*	0.0870*	0.0522	0.1025*	0.1689*	0.1362*	91,969
	(0.0050)	(0.0051)	(0.0052)	(0.0062)	(0.0073)	(0.0072)	(0.0085)	(0.0091)	
High school grads	0.0243*	0.0716*	0.0769*	0.0793	0.0414	0.1003*	0.1587*	0.1143*	157,633
	(0.0045)	(0.0048)	(0.0052)	(0.0050)	(0.0068)	(0.0070)	(0.0078)	(0.0071)	
Some college	0.0125*	0.0404*	0.0373	0.0389	0.0374	0.0572*	0.0895*	0.0613*	98,506
	(0.0049)	(0.0052)	(0.0046)	(0.0048)	(0.0083)	(0.0075)	(0.0084)	(0.0072)	
College grads	0.0131*	0.0306*	0.0316	0.0353	0.0200	0.0331	0.0576*	0.0551	102,189
	(0.0045)	(0.0051)	(0.0043)	(0.0050)	(0.0069)	(0.0075)	(0.0082)	(0.0080)	
Women by Education Level:									
High school dropouts	0.0056	0.0409*	0.0393	0.0456	0.0318	0.0593*	0.0872*	0.0490*	61,124
	(0.0047)	(0.0049)	(0.0049)	(0.0060)	(0.0073)	(0.0071)	(0.0082)	(0.0081)	
High school grads	0.0124*	0.0289*	0.0307	0.0327	0.0144	0.0488*	0.0614*	0.0411*	158,721
	(0.0033)	(0.0032)	(0.0030)	(0.0034)	(0.0047)	(0.0049)	(0.0050)	(0.0046)	
Some college	0.0112*	0.0244*	0.0182*	0.0170	0.0287	0.0357	0.0382	0.0307	88,716
	(0.0055)	(0.0052)	(0.0044)	(0.0044)	(0.0090)	(0.0075)	(0.0070)	(0.0063)	
College grads	0.0102*	0.0191*	0.0107*	0.0137	0.0125	0.0219	0.0289	0.0183*	72,904
	(0.0054)	(0.0052)	(0.0044)	(0.0042)	(0.0083)	(0.0075)	(0.0070)	(0.0059)	
Men by Years of Potential Experience:									
1 - 10 years	0.0336*	0.0676*	0.0549*	0.0513*	0.0469	0.1058*	0.1347*	0.0886*	151,281
	(0.0047)	(0.0044)	(0.0040)	(0.0045)	(0.0070)	(0.0069)	(0.0069)	(0.0065)	
11 - 20 years	0.0133*	0.0724*	0.0779*	0.0786	0.0473	0.0745*	0.1602*	0.1076*	127,307
	(0.0042)	(0.0054)	(0.0046)	(0.0051)	(0.0073)	(0.0072)	(0.0092)	(0.0076)	
21 - 30 years	0.0199*	0.0541*	0.0737*	0.0775	0.0257	0.0627*	0.1139*	0.1146	97,705
	(0.0042)	(0.0052)	(0.0051)	(0.0054)	(0.0060)	(0.0069)	(0.0089)	(0.0089)	
31 - 40 years	0.0078*	0.0420*	0.0559*	0.0586	0.0203	0.0515*	0.1007*	0.0960	74,004
	(0.0038)	(0.0049)	(0.0051)	(0.0059)	(0.0059)	(0.0065)	(0.0090)	(0.0096)	

Table 1 (continued)

Women by Years of Potential Experience:	Expansion Years				Recession Years				Observations
	1971 - 73	1976 - 80	1983 - 89	1992 - 97	1970	1974 - 75	1981 - 82	1990 - 91	
1 - 10 years	0.0150*	0.0342*	0.0265*	0.0242	0.0271	0.0532*	0.0588	0.0350*	132,041
	(0.0040)	(0.0037)	(0.0037)	(0.0061)	(0.0061)	(0.0056)	(0.0054)	(0.0050)	
11 - 20 years	0.0083*	0.0321*	0.0322	0.0330	0.0260	0.0372	0.0637*	0.0419*	105,272
	(0.0041)	(0.0044)	(0.0037)	(0.0041)	(0.0067)	(0.0061)	(0.0056)	(0.0056)	
21 - 30 years	0.0013	0.0205*	0.0200	0.0276*	0.0100	0.0288*	0.0512*	0.0382*	83,869
	(0.0032)	(0.0037)	(0.0033)	(0.0036)	(0.0050)	(0.0053)	(0.0063)	(0.0056)	
31 - 40 years	0.0095*	0.0204*	0.0203	0.0206	0.0087	0.0419*	0.0385	0.0269*	60,283
	(0.0039)	(0.0040)	(0.0038)	(0.0042)	(0.0054)	(0.0053)	(0.0064)	(0.0062)	
All Workers by Industry Group:									
Goods producing	0.0200*	0.0631*	0.0699*	0.0722	0.0474*	0.0977*	0.1487*	0.1056*	261,885
	(0.0029)	(0.0031)	(0.0030)	(0.0034)	(0.0046)	(0.0046)	(0.0052)	(0.0050)	
Services producing	0.0135*	0.0342*	0.0335	0.0364	0.0186	0.0409*	0.0629*	0.0509*	569,877
	(0.0017)	(0.0018)	(0.0016)	(0.0018)	(0.0025)	(0.0026)	(0.0028)	(0.0026)	
All Workers by Occupation Group:									
White collar	-	0.0110*	0.0097	0.0133*	0.0059	0.0159*	0.0257*	0.0222	418,571
		(0.0013)	(0.0012)	(0.0013)	(0.0020)	(0.0019)	(0.0021)	(0.0020)	
Blue collar	-	0.0476*	0.0548*	0.0511*	0.0203	0.0753*	0.1270*	0.0826*	252,949
		(0.0029)	(0.0028)	(0.0031)	(0.0041)	(0.0042)	(0.0048)	(0.0046)	
Service	-	0.0273*	0.0291	0.0247	0.0087	0.0326*	0.0694*	0.0355*	91,078
		(0.0042)	(0.0038)	(0.0040)	(0.0060)	(0.0059)	(0.0067)	(0.0057)	

Note: Each line contains the results from a separate probit equation for the indicated group. The dependent variable equals one if the individual made an EU transition. All coefficients are expressed as marginal effects (relative to the 1967 period). The regressions include the following control variables (where appropriate): sex, non white, a set of experience dummies, a set of education dummies, and the percentage change in real GDP.

* Significantly different from the previous period of the same type (that is, the coefficient to the left) at the 5% level. Note that the 1970 recession period is not compared to a previous recession period because the last recession is not covered by the data.

Figure 9: Comparison to Boisjoly, Duncan, and Smeeding(1998): Job Loss Rates from the PSID and EU Transition Rates from the March CPS

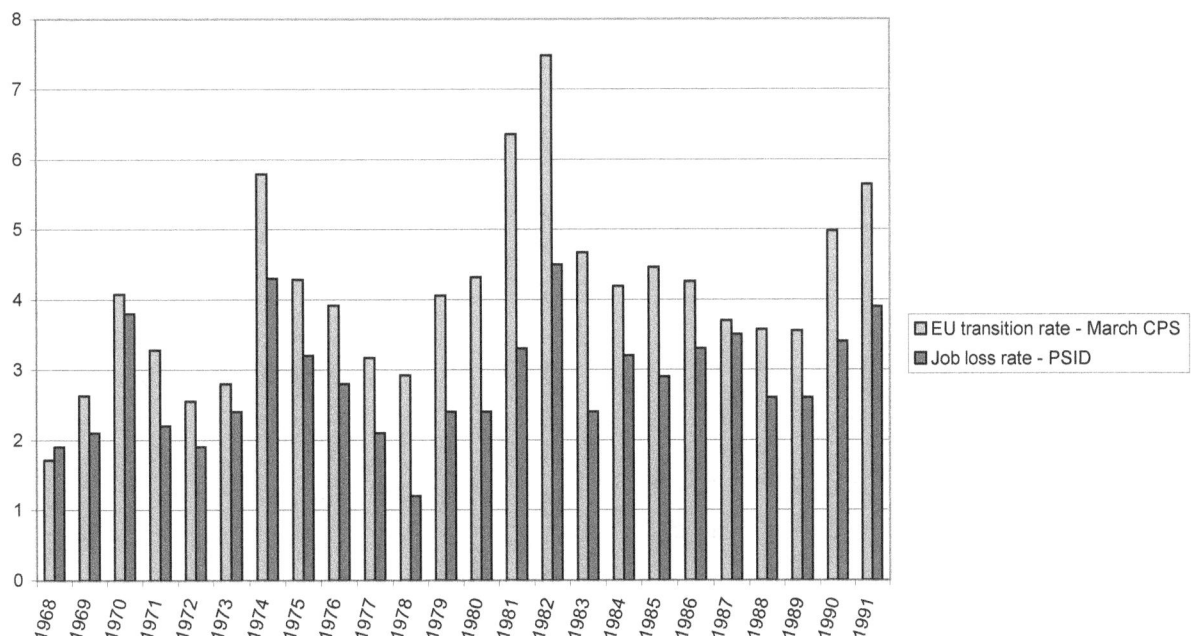

Note: The PSID data are from Boisjoly, Duncan, and Smeeding (1998)

Figure 10: Comparison to Farber (1997a): Job Loss Rates from the DWS and EU Transition Rates from the March CPS

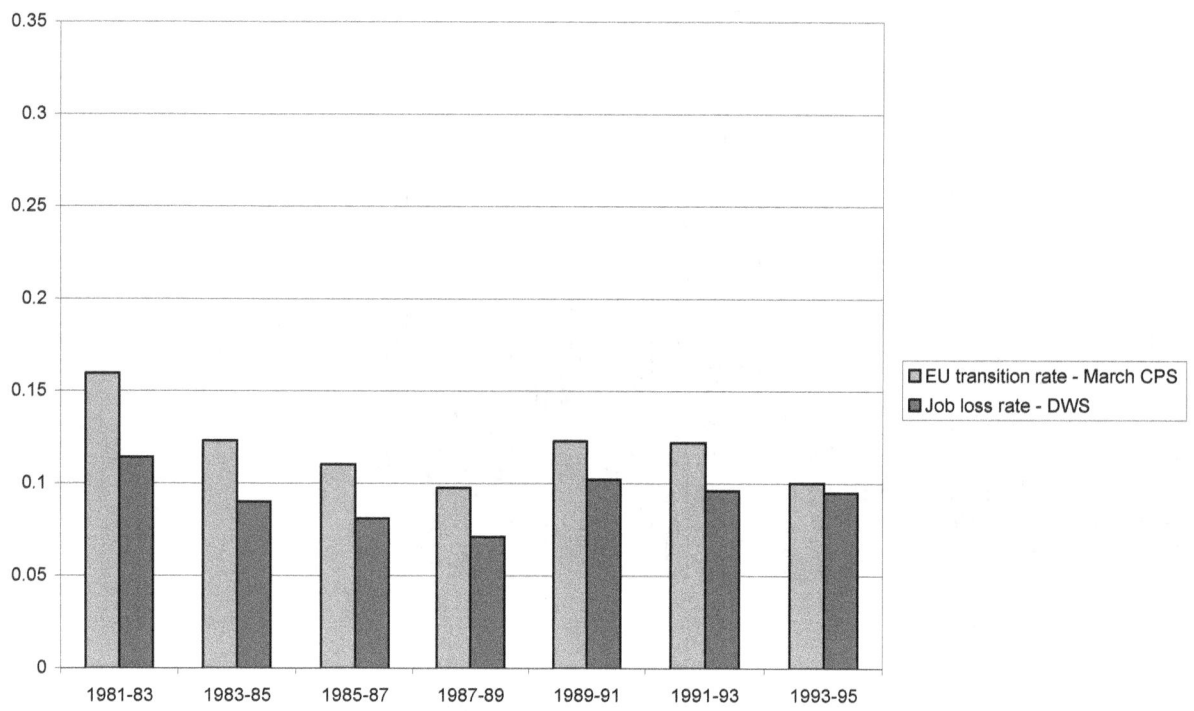

Note: The DWS data are from Farber (1997a).

Table 2: Estimated Lower Bounds on the Change in the Reemployment Rate for Job Losers Between the 1991-93 and 1993-95 Periods

Initial Values (1991-93 period)				Change between the 1991-93 and 1993-95 periods				
P_L	P_{LU}	P_{LN}	P_{LE}	ΔP_L	ΔP_{LU}	ΔP_{LN}	ΔP_{LE}	$\Delta P_{LE}/P_{LE}$
9.60	2.74	0.00	6.86	-0.10	-0.64	0.00	0.54	7.86
9.60	2.74	0.50	6.36	-0.10	-0.64	0.00	0.54	8.47
9.60	2.74	1.00	5.86	-0.10	-0.64	0.00	0.54	9.20
9.60	2.74	1.50	5.36	-0.10	-0.64	0.00	0.54	10.05
9.60	2.74	2.00	4.86	-0.10	-0.64	0.00	0.54	11.09

Note: The data have been adjusted to account for recall bias and the CPS redesign.

Table 3: Comparison to Monks and Pizer (1998): Probit Equations on Job Loss in the NLS and EU Transitions in the March CPS

	White		Nonwhite	
	March CPS	NLS	March CPS	NLS
Time trend interacted with:				
High school dropout	0.0141***	0.0182***	0.0218***	0.0135*
	(0.0028)	(0.0060)	(0.0065)	(0.0077)
High school graduate	0.0090***	0.0126**	0.0094**	0.0206***
	(0.0022)	(0.0053)	(0.0053)	(0.0076)
Some college	0.0019	0.0194***	0.0080	0.0097
	(0.0029)	(0.0063)	(0.0075)	(0.0101)
College graduate	0.0019	0.0138**	-0.0166	0.0217
	(0.0040)	(0.0063)	(0.0115)	(0.0167)
Number of observations	53,053	14,551	6,541	5,442

Note: The NLS results are from Monks and Pizer (1998). The dependent variables equal one if the individual made an EU transition (March CPS) or involuntarily left a job (NLS). The regressions include the following control variables: a set of education dummies, the unemployment rate, age, marital status, and industry and occupation dummies.

* Significant at the 10% level
** Significant at the 5% level
*** Significant at the 1% level

Table 4: Comparison to Monks and Pizer: Implied changes in Job Loss and EU Transition Rates

White	March CPS (EU transitions)			NLS (job loss)		
Education level:	Probability in 1971	1971-90 change	Percentage change	Probability in 1971	1971-90 change	Percentage change
High school dropout	3.8	2.9	76	9.9	7.4	75
High school graduate	2.5	1.2	48	7.1	3.8	54
Some college	2.4	0.3	13	5.4	5.4	100
College graduate	1.8	0.2	11	5.4	3.5	65
Nonwhite						
Education level:						
High school dropout	5.8	6.6	114	14.8	6.7	45
High school graduate	4.5	2.0	44	10.4	8.9	86
Some college	3.9	1.5	38	10.1	3.7	37
College graduate	5.5	-2.7	-49	3.1	4.2	135

Note: These changes were computed using the coefficients fro the probit equations in Table 3. Steve Pizer kindly provided the percentages from the NLS.